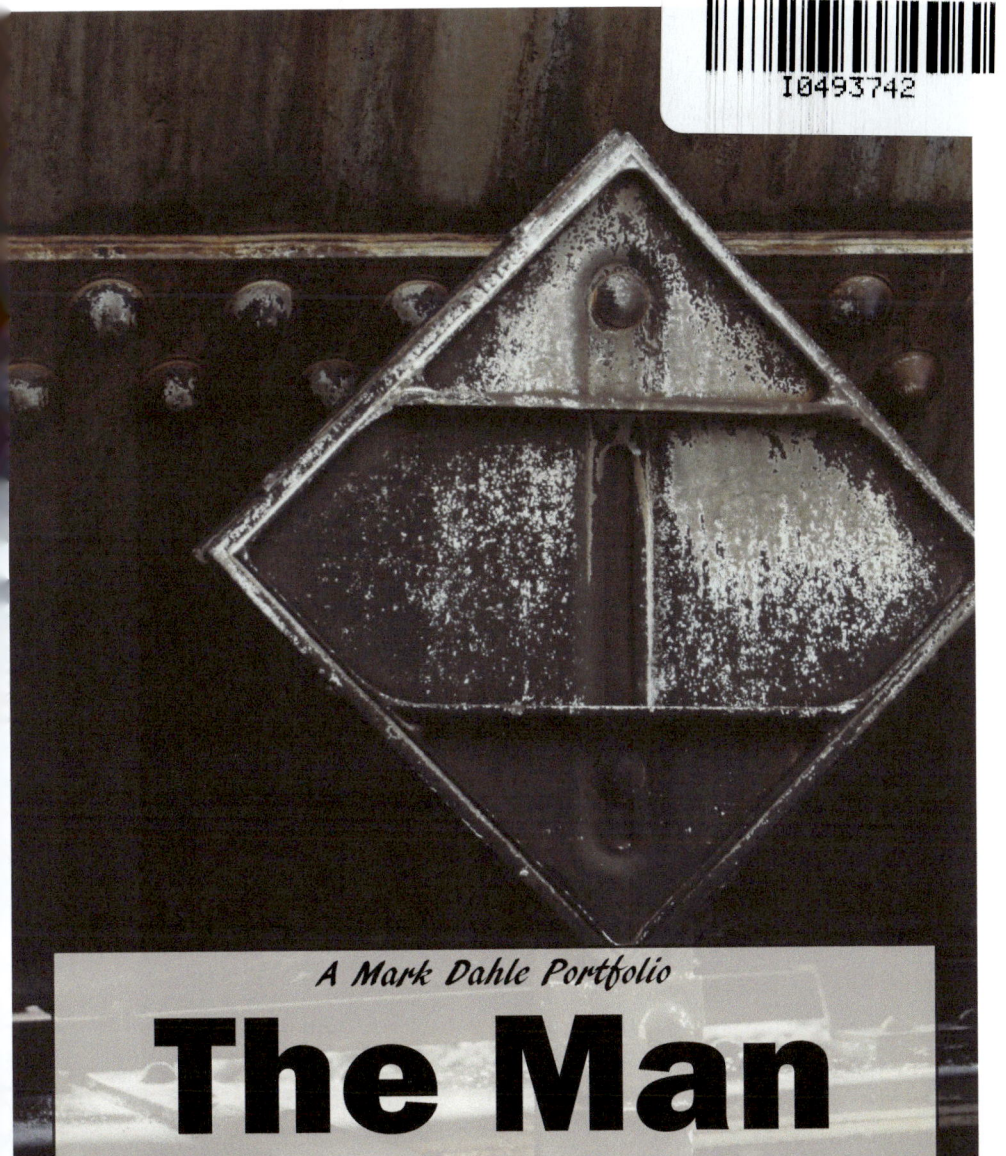

A Mark Dahle Portfolio

The Man Who Liked To Dream

Mark Dahle Portfolios can be read in a few minutes and enjoyed for a lifetime.

Mark Dahle Portfolios combine text with beautiful photographs and a painting. Unlike many picture books, the text is unrelated to the art. This might seem a little weird at first. One thing that helps is to order more portfolios until you get used to it. In the meantime, feel free to draw your own pictures of the stories on the pages.

This portfolio includes three very short commentaries (The Man Who Liked To Dream, Hiking To The Middle, and Disappointment), a photo of a brilliant 36 x 24 inch abstract painting (at the right) and twenty-seven beautiful industrial photographs of Redding, CA.

Photographs in this book are available in limited editions. See http://www.MarkDahle.com for more information and for previews of upcoming portfolios.

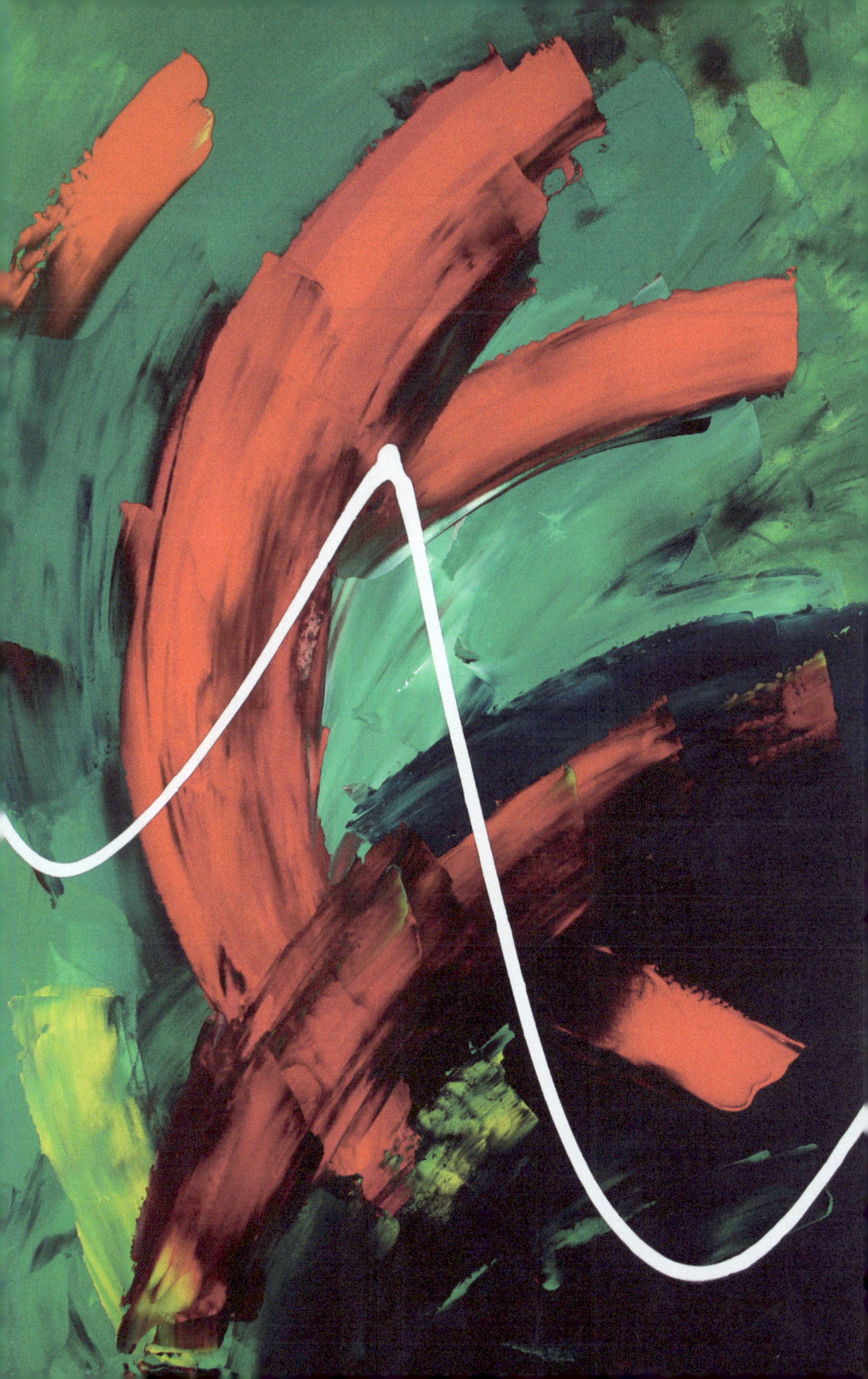

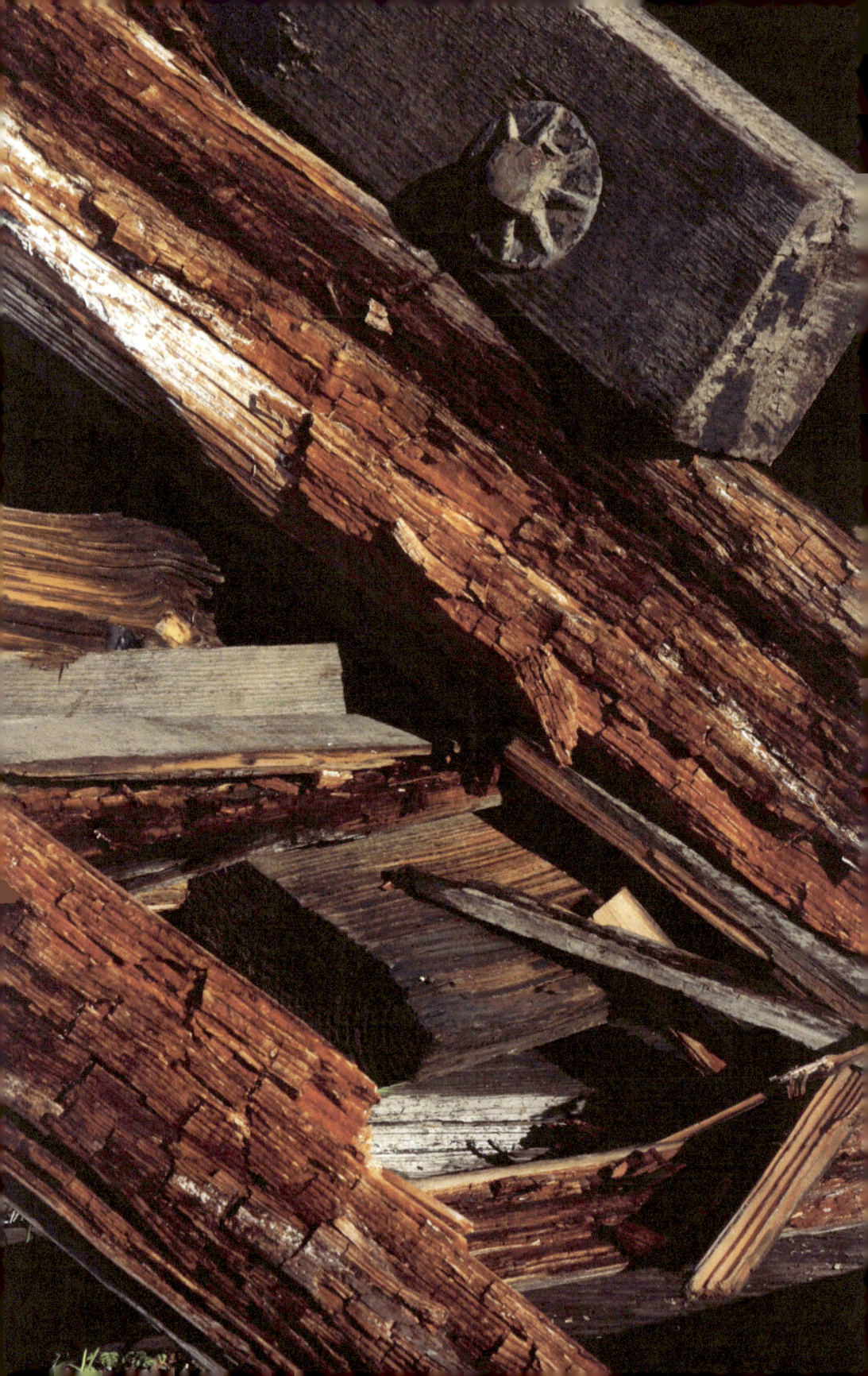

The Man Who Liked To Dream

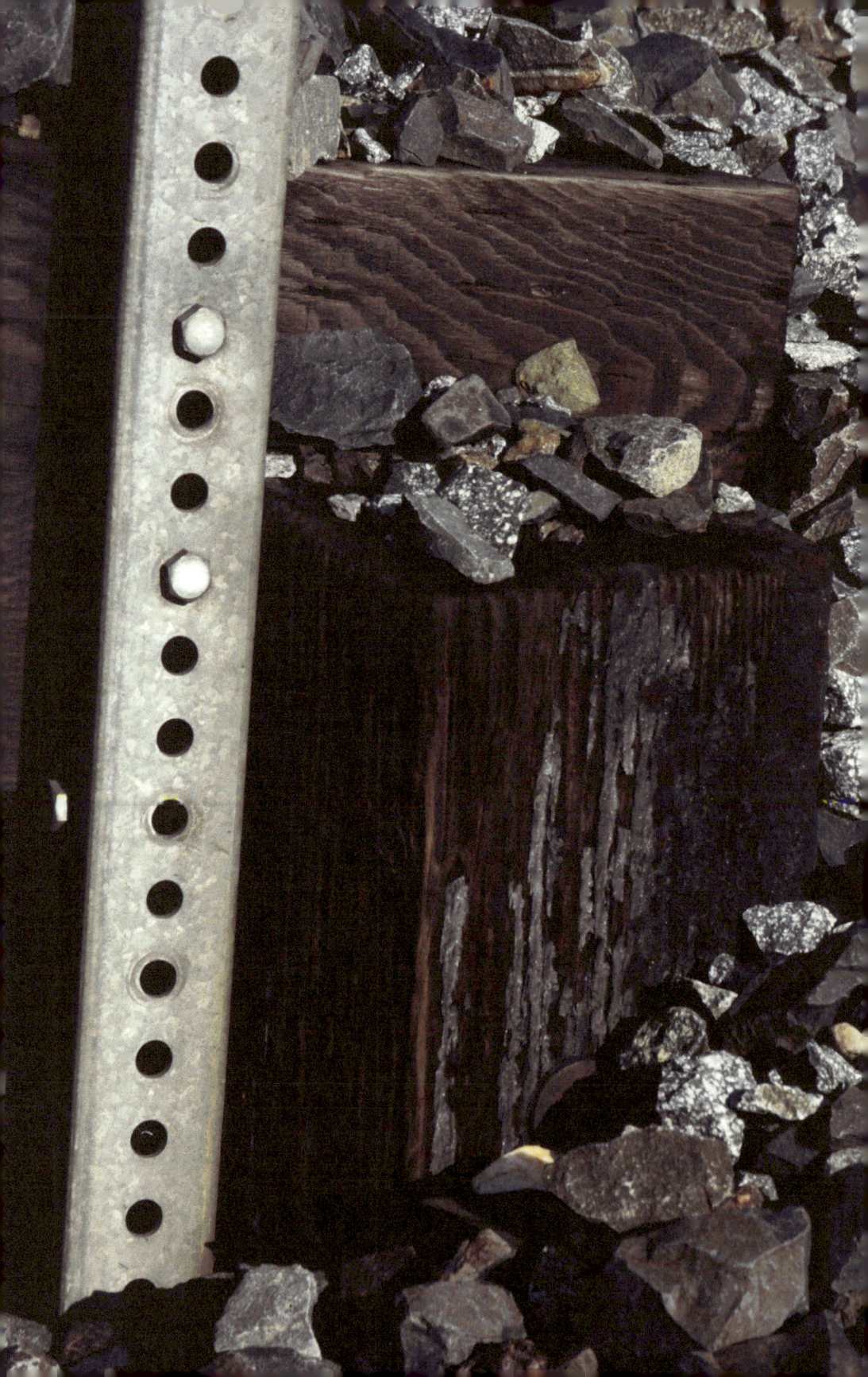

Once there was a man
who knew exactly what he wanted.

His name was Fred.

He had everything he wanted
all planned out.

He could picture it
when he closed his eyes.

So that's what he did.

He lay down on his bed
and closed his eyes
every chance he could.

He would do this
for days at a time.

It was awesome.

When he closed his eyes,
he had everything.

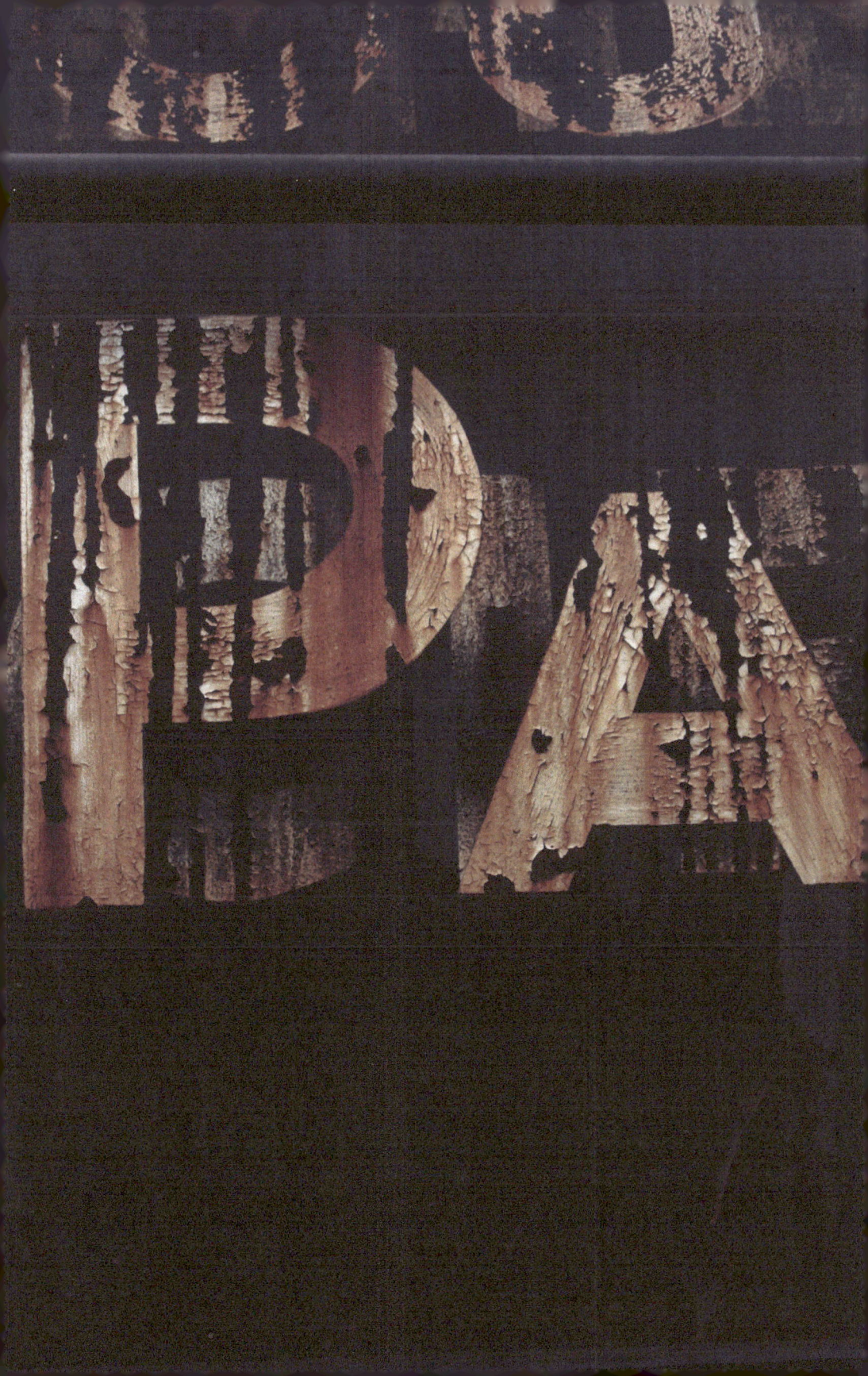

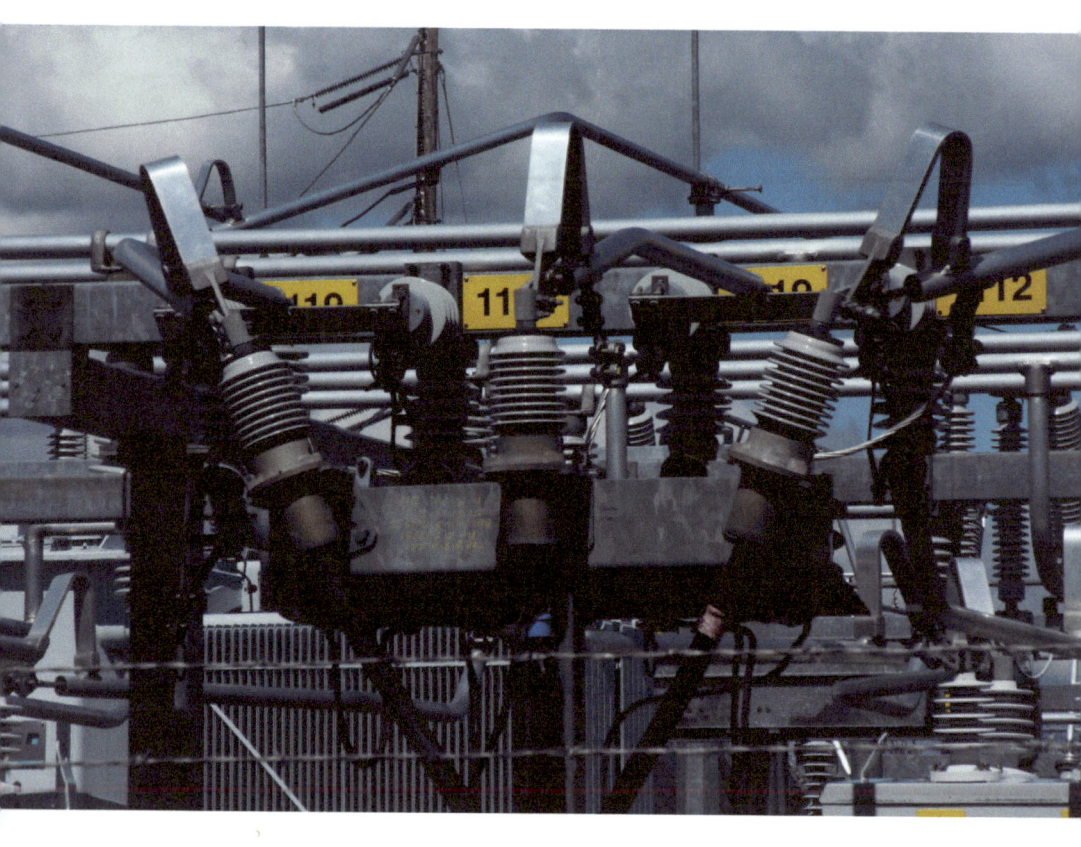

It was not awesome
when he opened his eyes.

When he opened his eyes,
nothing was right.

But when he closed his eyes,
which he did a lot,
everything was perfect.

Fred was very happy,
lying still
and picturing what he wanted.

Fred had a friend.
Her name was Martha.

By coincidence,
Martha wanted the same things
that Fred did.

But Martha never lay down
and closed her eyes
unless she had to.

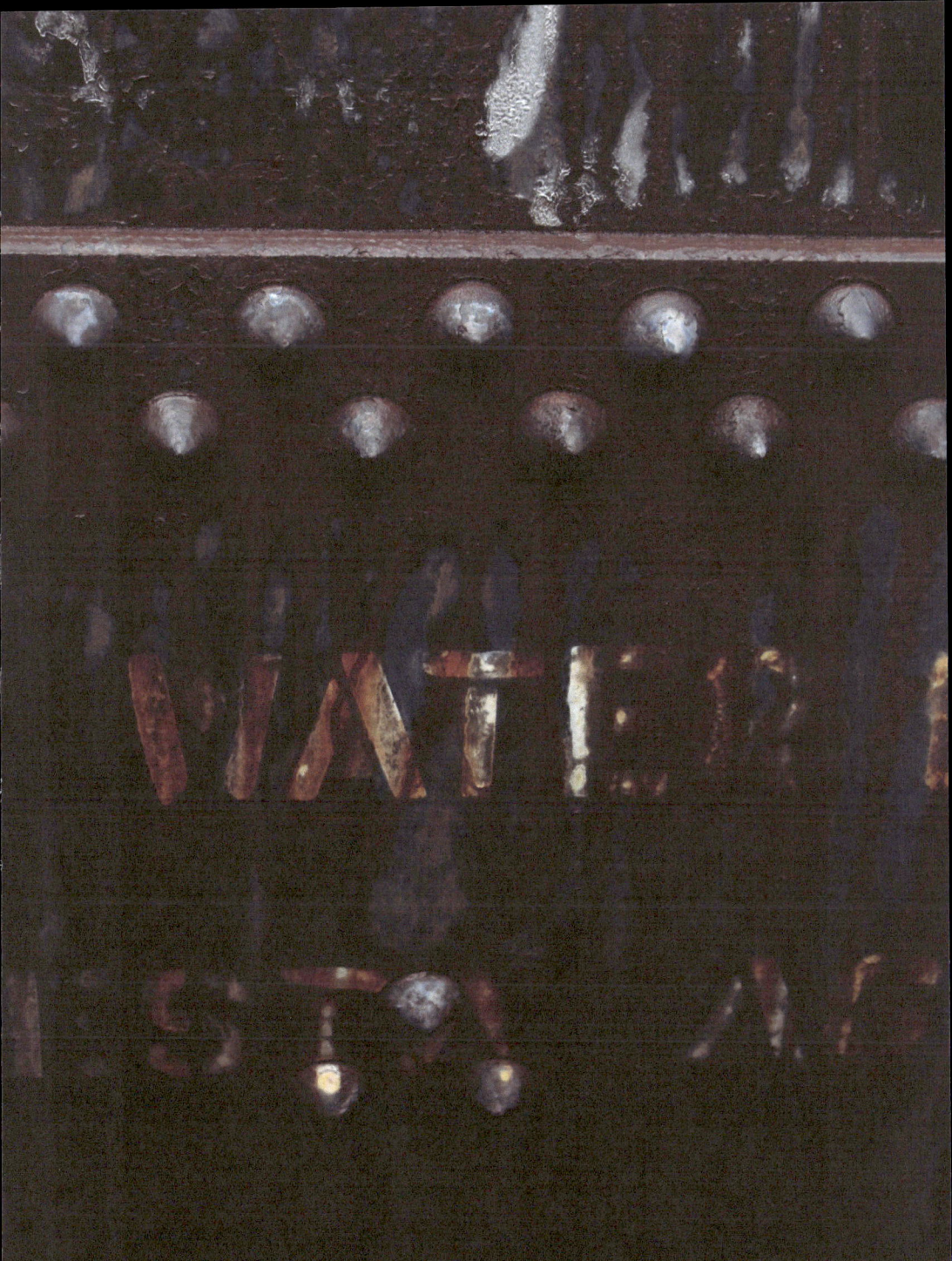

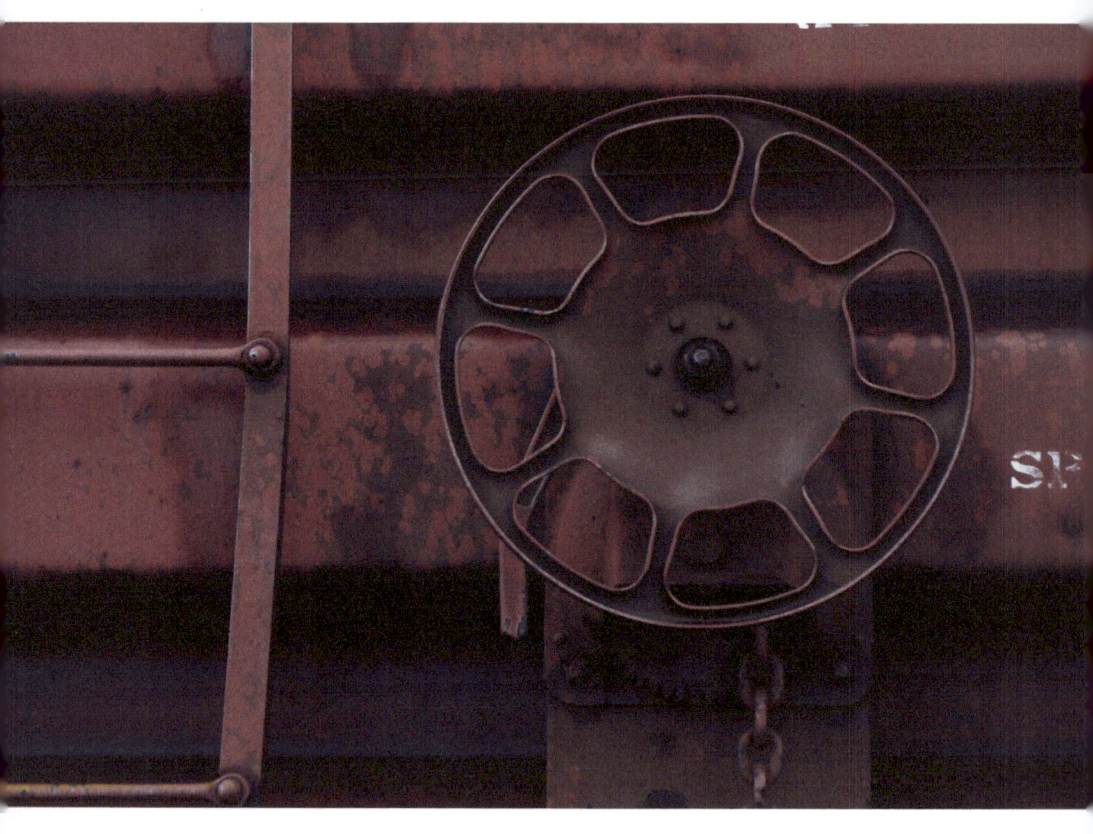

Instead of closing her eyes
and picturing what she wanted,
Martha opened her eyes and went to work.

As it turned out,
Martha got what she wanted.
And Fred got lots of naps.

~ ~ ~

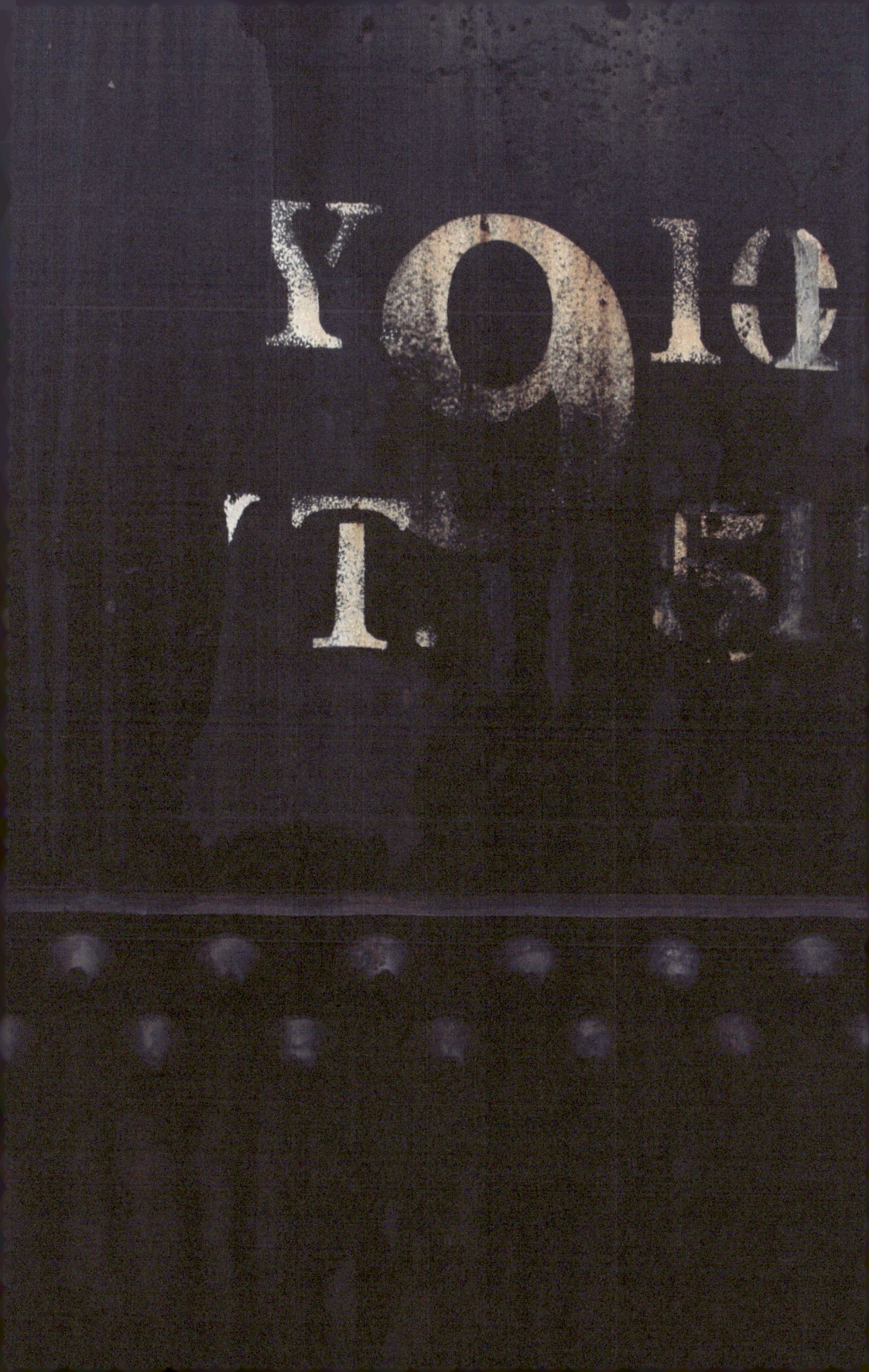

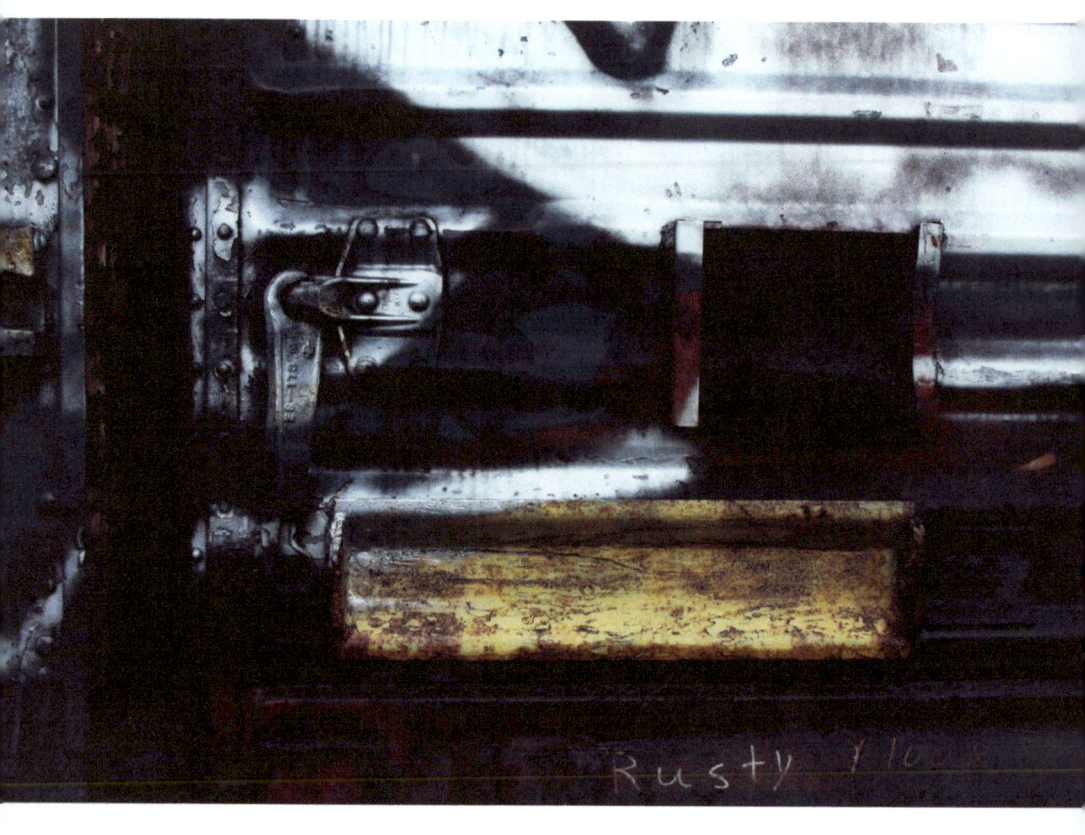

Hiking To The Middle

Some people never leave their homes to go hiking.

Some people *do* leave their homes,
but when they get to a view area,
they just drive by it.

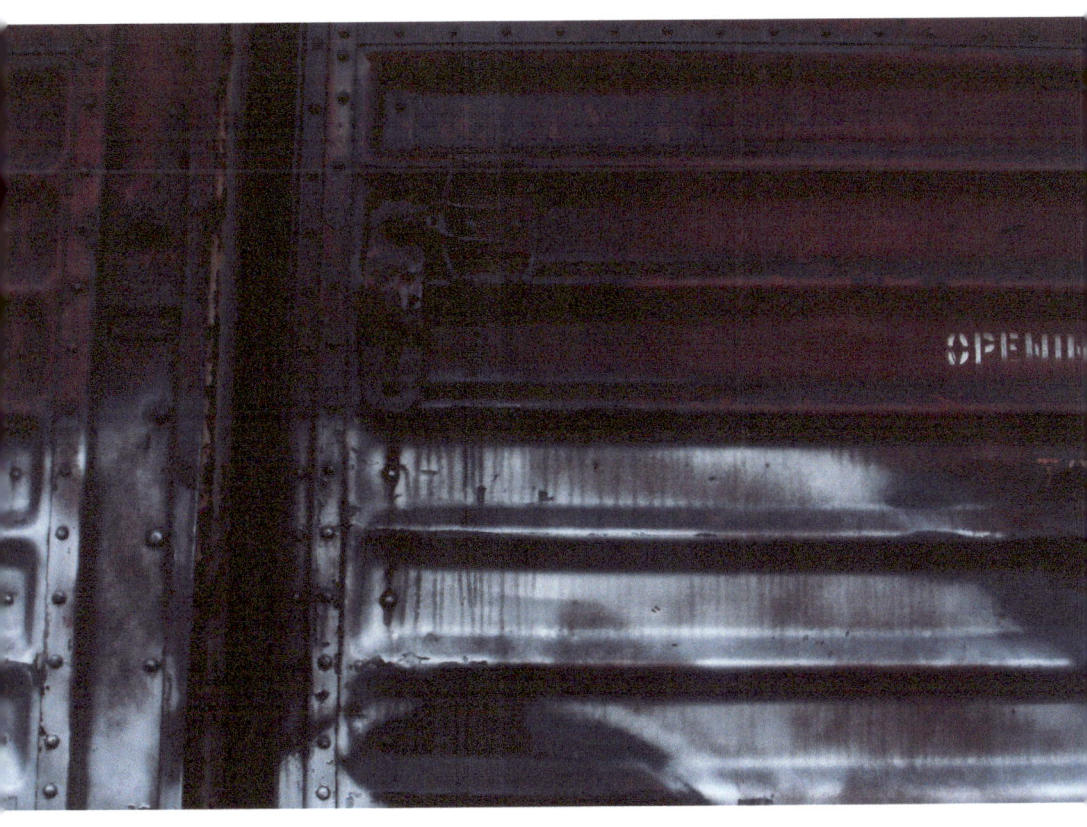

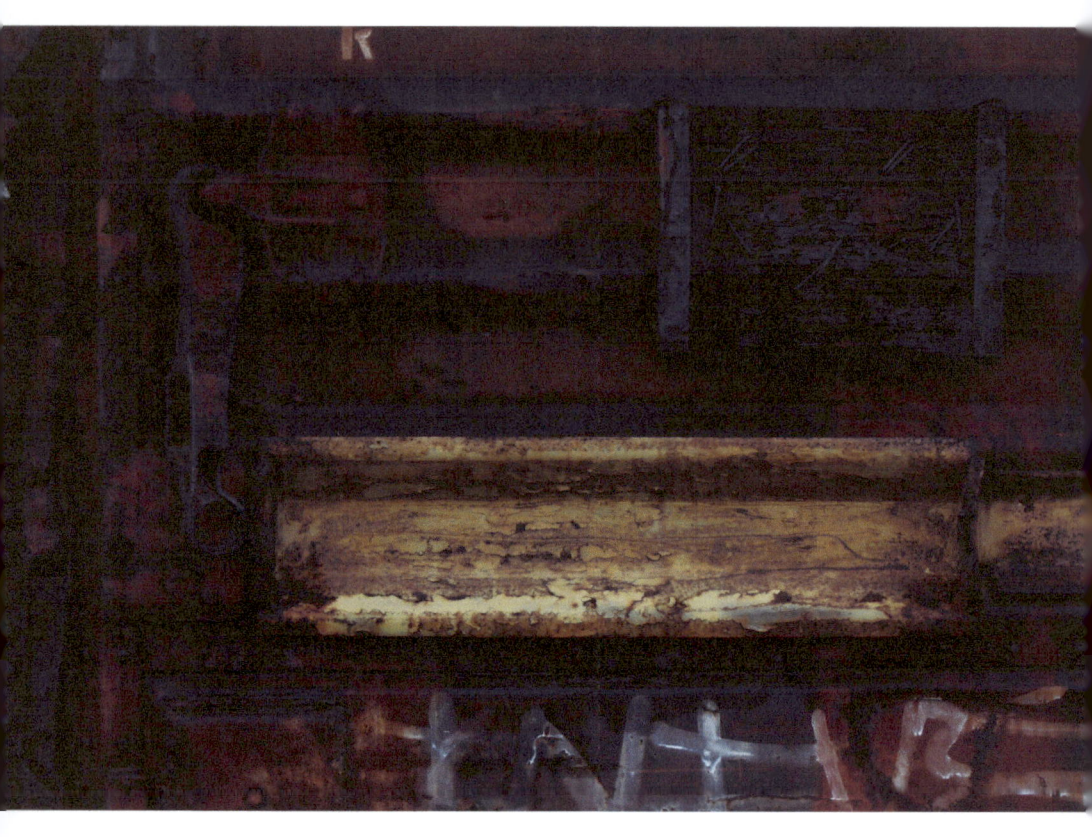

Some people drive to a base camp
with their RVs,
TVs
and radios
and never go outside.

Some people actually get out
and go for a short stroll
on the cement sidewalk,
but they don't go any farther
than that.

There are *lots* of people who don't go hiking.

But for the moment
let's just pay attention
to the people
who actually *do* go hiking.

Of that group,
do you know anyone who says,
"Hey, let's go
to the middle
of the mountain?"

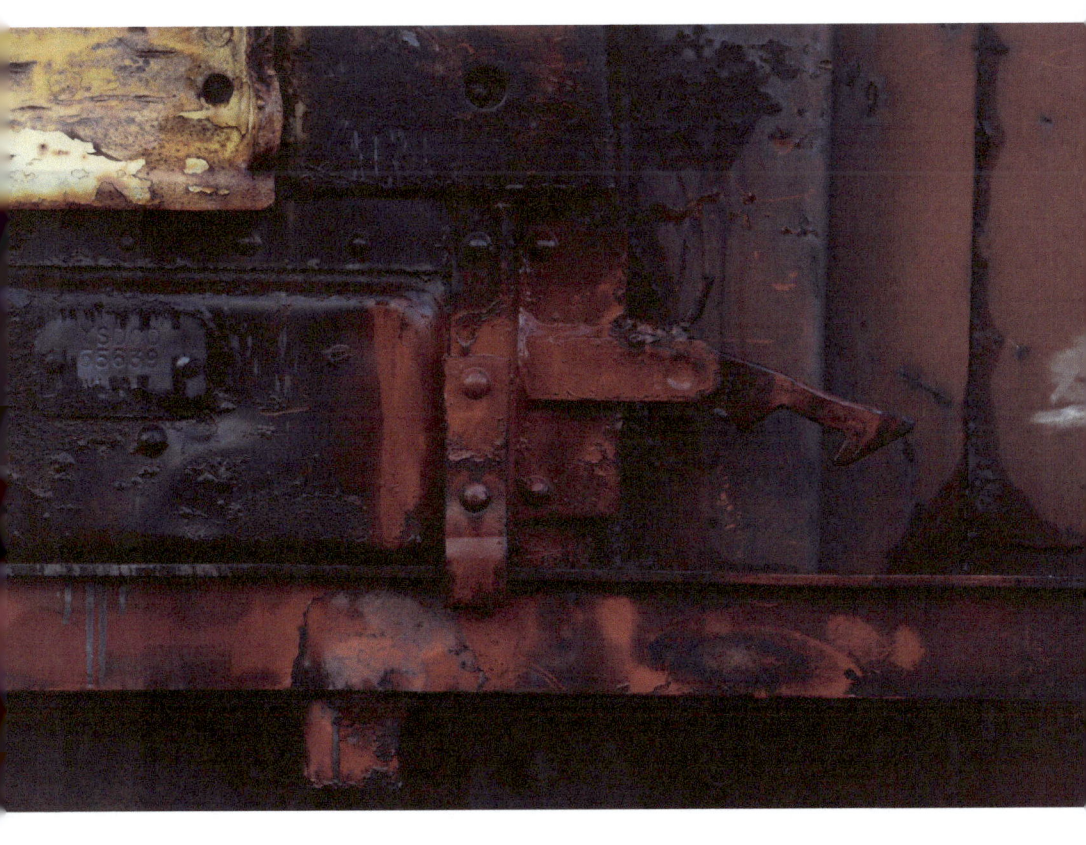

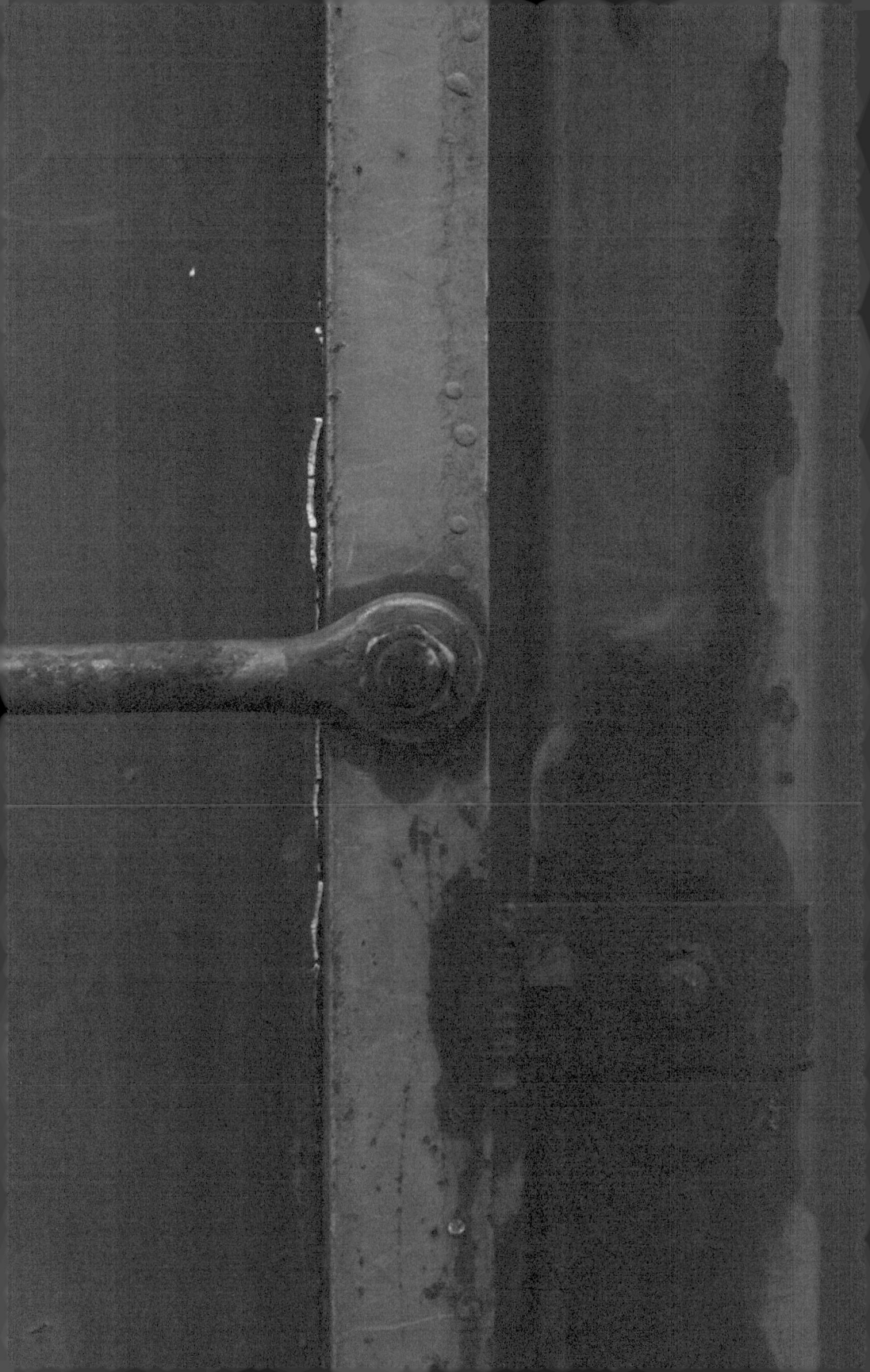

I don't know anybody like that, either.

If nobody ever says that,
how come so many of us
stop half way in our quests
and never get
to where the view is magnificant,
the air grand,
the flowers wild,
and the experience
overwhelming?

Why do so many of us
stop at the middle of the mountain?

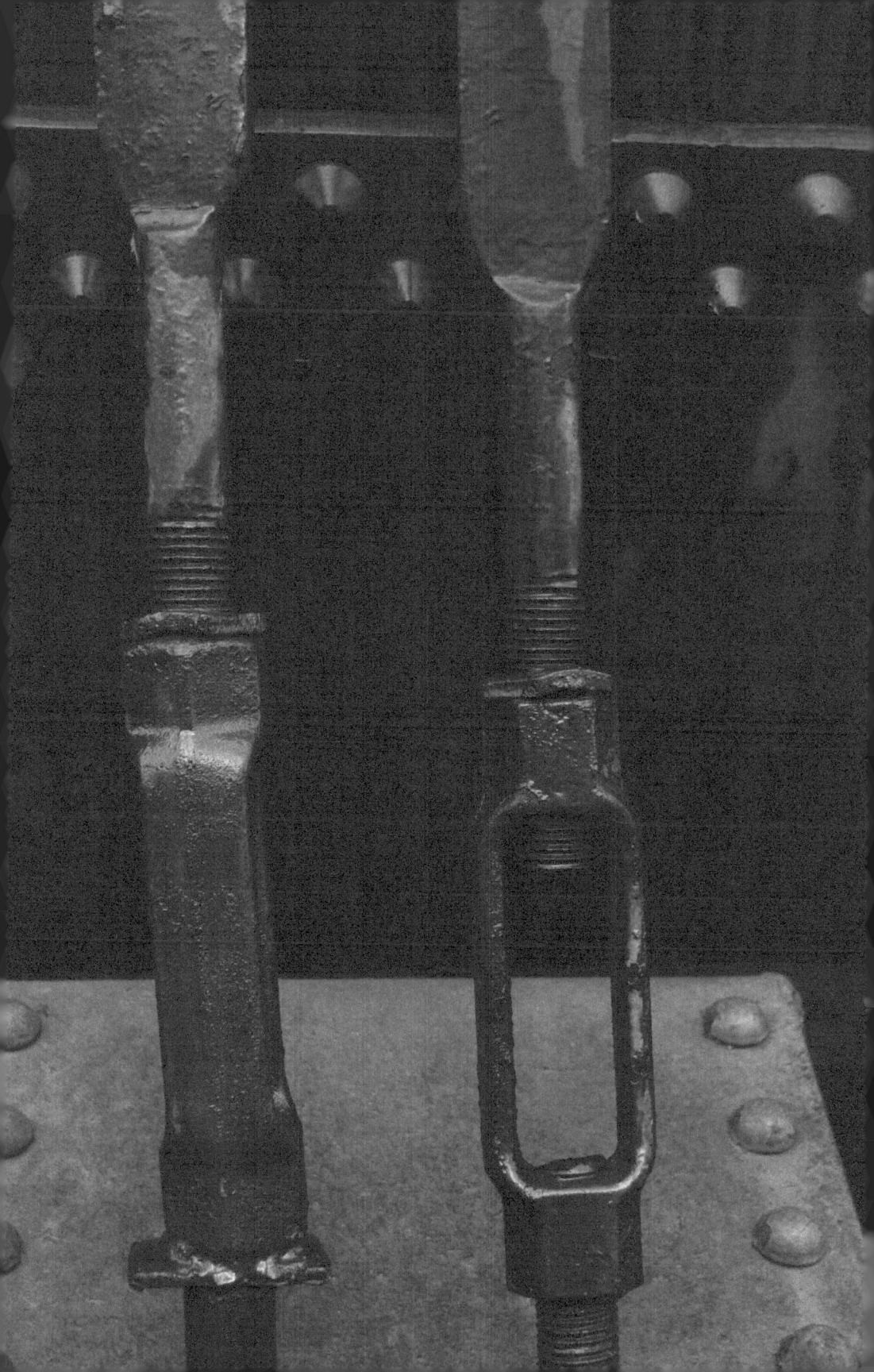

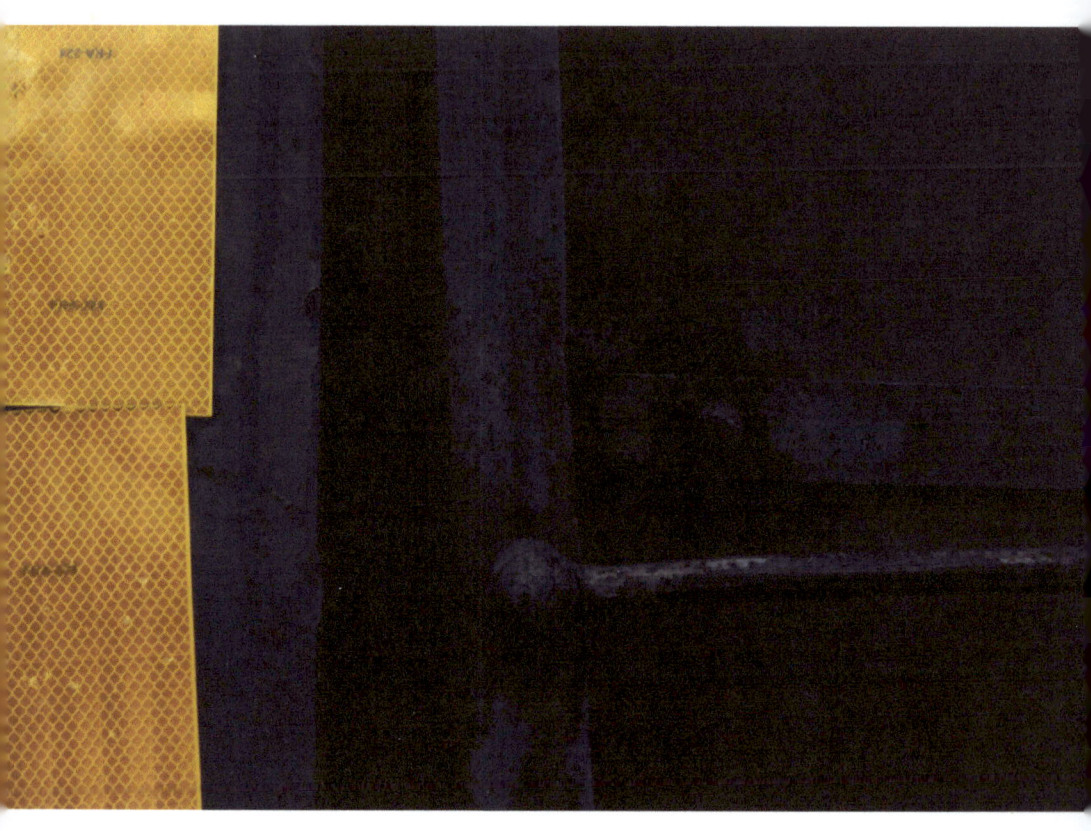

And where,
if it's not too impolite to ask,
where on the mountain are *you*?

~ ~ ~

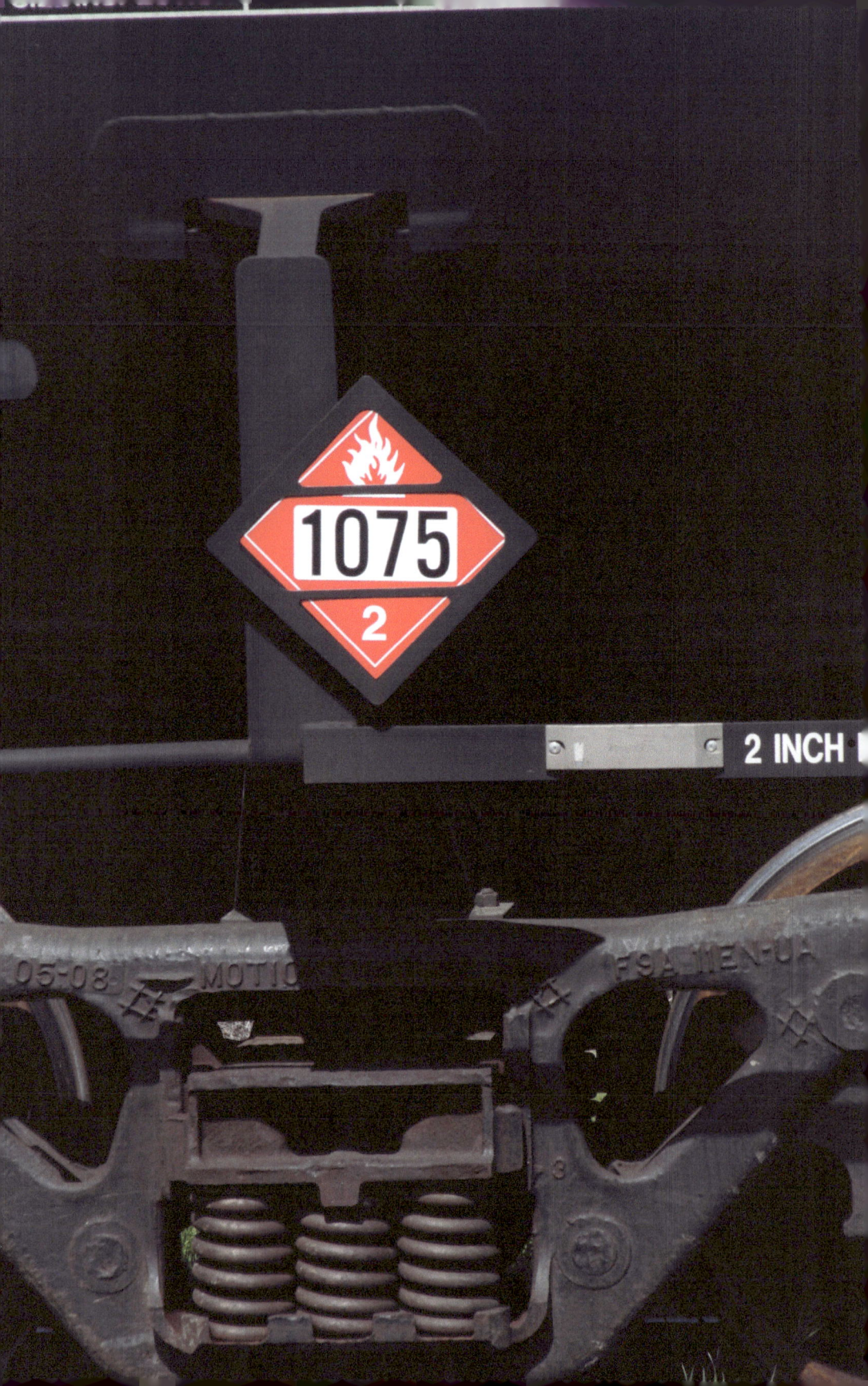

Disappointed

Sam was *so* disappointed in his airplane ride.

Everything was still the same.
What a letdown after all the planning!

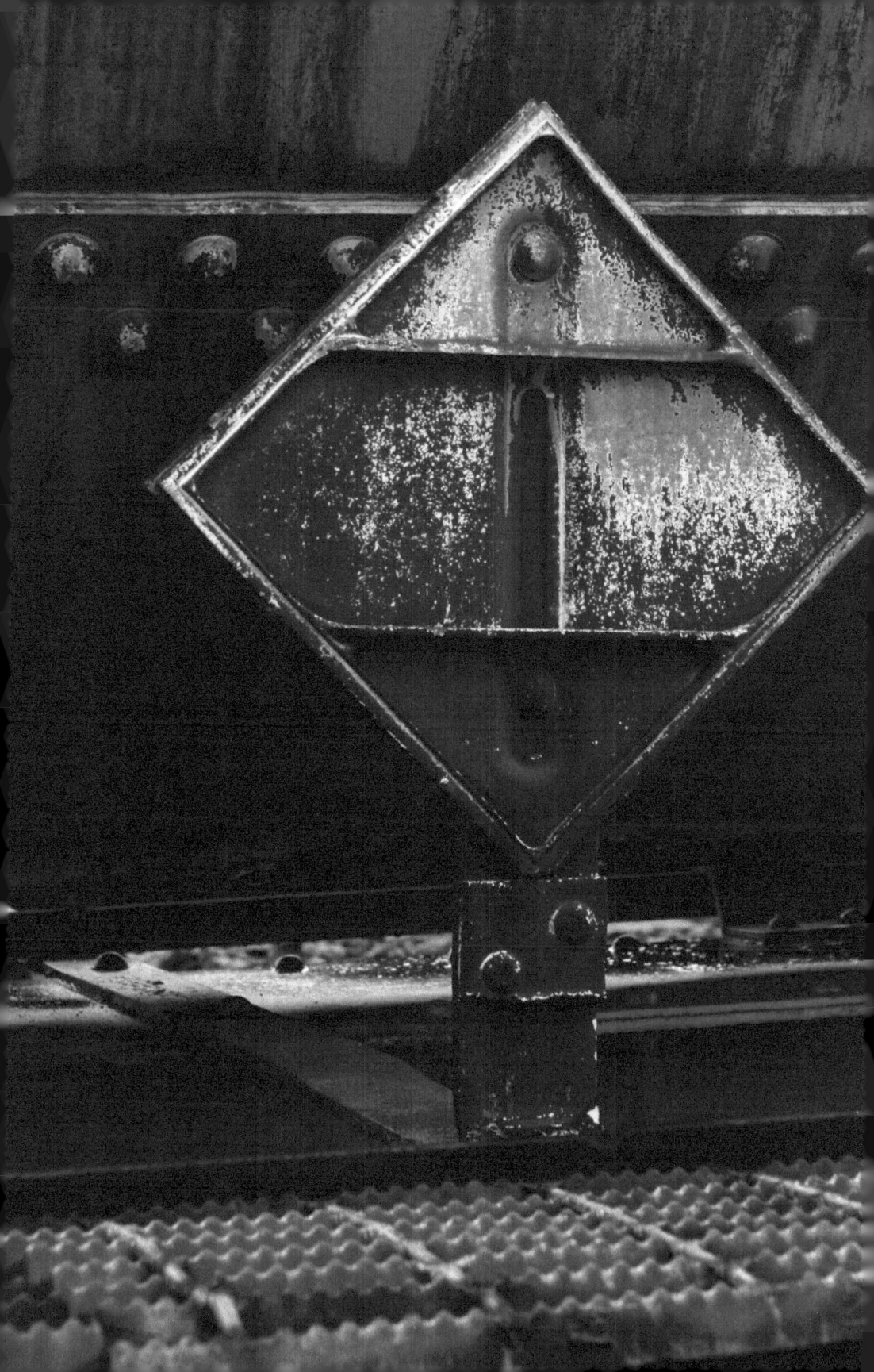

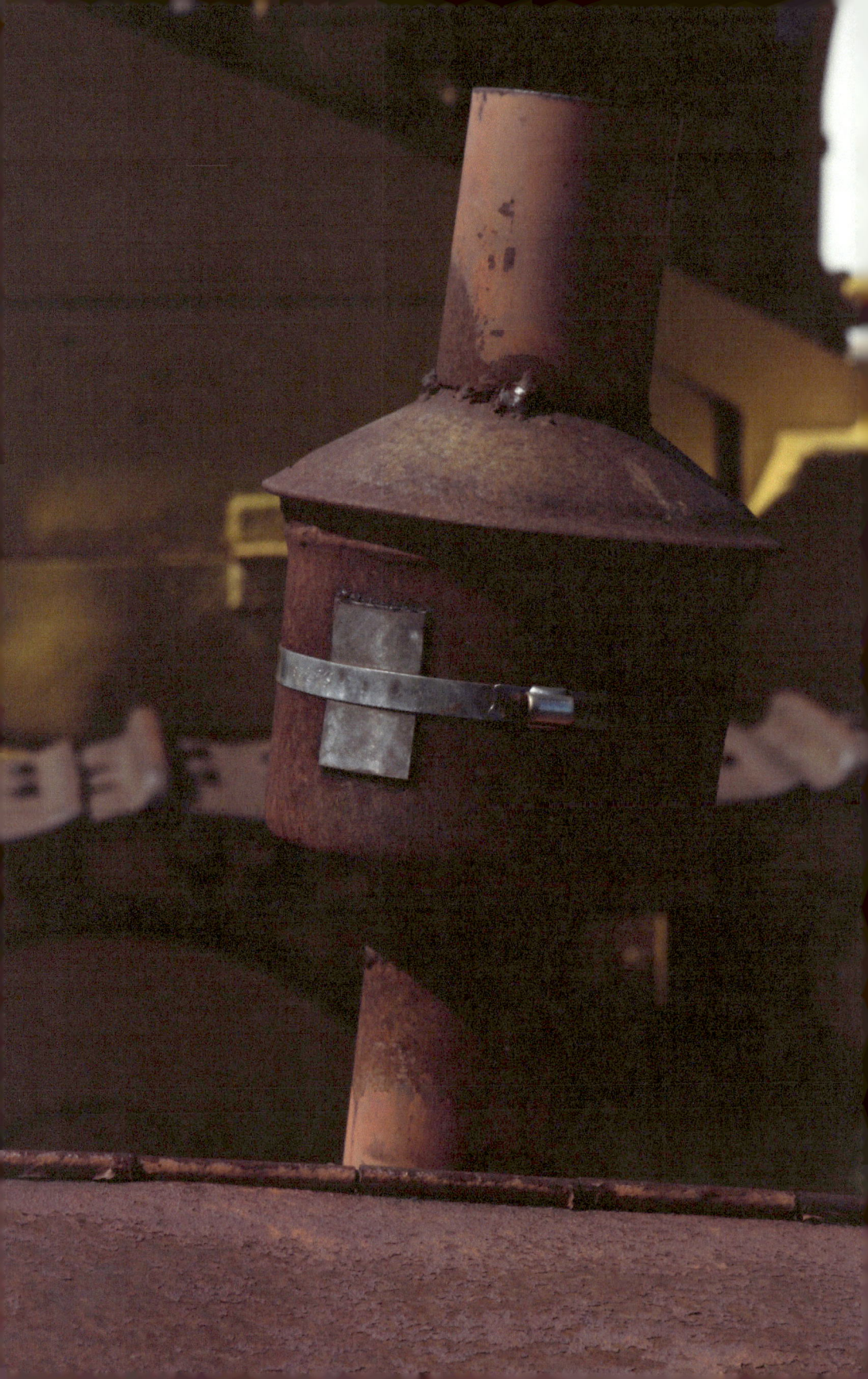

At first, Sam hadn't wanted to take an airplane ride.
Sam took a long time to think about it.
You know: Weighing the cost.
Considering the options.
Comparing the possibilities.

But eventually Sam bought a ticket.

The day of Sam's flight,
he got to the airport early,
checked in,
went through security,
and got on the plane.

When all the passengers were aboard,
the plane taxied to the runway.
It took off slowly
but quickly gained altitude once it was in the air.

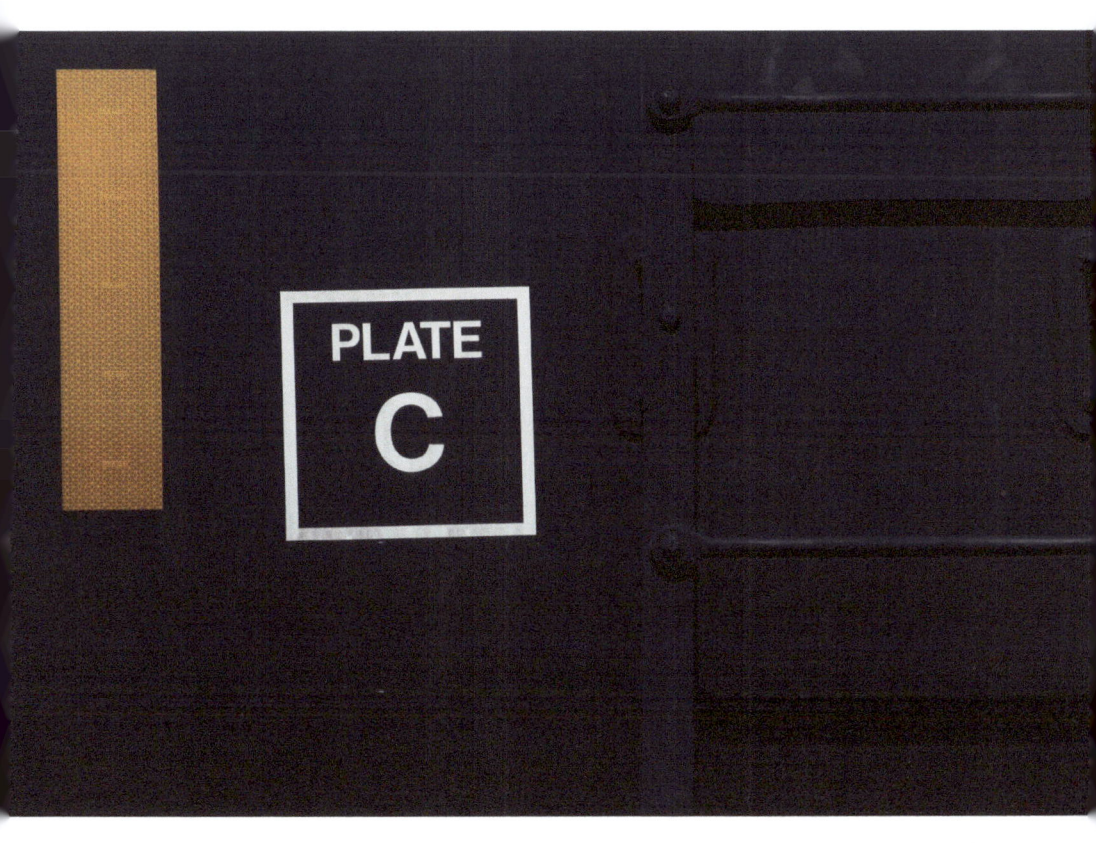

PLATE
C

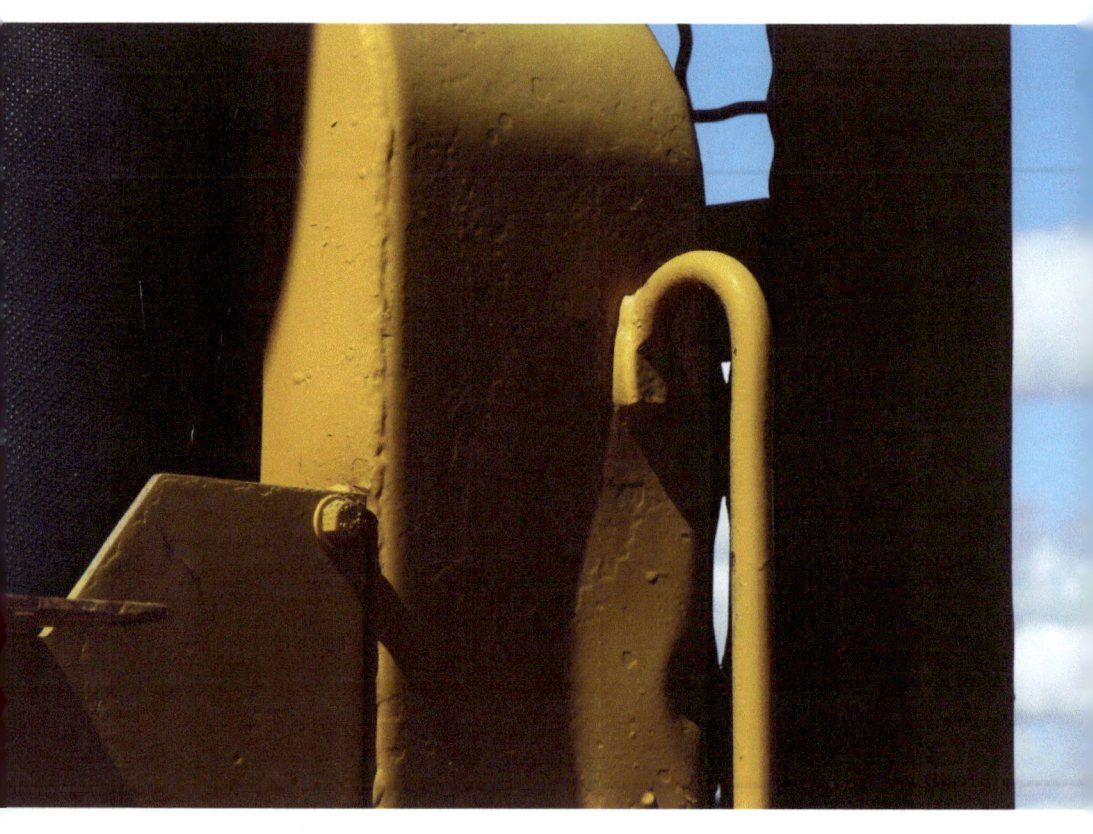

At 10,000 feet the seatbelt sign went off.
Sam was free to move about the cabin.
Sam got a meal.
Sam watched a movie.
Sam took a nap.
Sam took out the airplane magazine
and filled in half of the crossword puzzle.
Sam walked to the restroom.
Sam talked to a flight attendant.
Eventually the plane started to descend.
At 10,000 feet the seatbelt sign came back on.

Sam buckled his seatbelt.
The plane got lower and lower.
The wheels touched the ground.
The plane slowed,
then taxied to the airport.

Wow!
Was Sam ever disappointed!
Everything was the same!

DOT 112J340W

	STATION STENCIL	QUALIFIED	DUE
TANK QUALIFICATION	TIOC	2008	2018
THICKNESS TEST	TIOC	2008	2018
SERVICE EQUIPMENT	TIOC	2008	2013
PRD: VALVE 280.5PSI	TIOC	2008	2013
LINING			
88.B.2 INSPECTION	TIOC	2008	2018
STUB SILL INSPECTION	TIOC	2008	2018

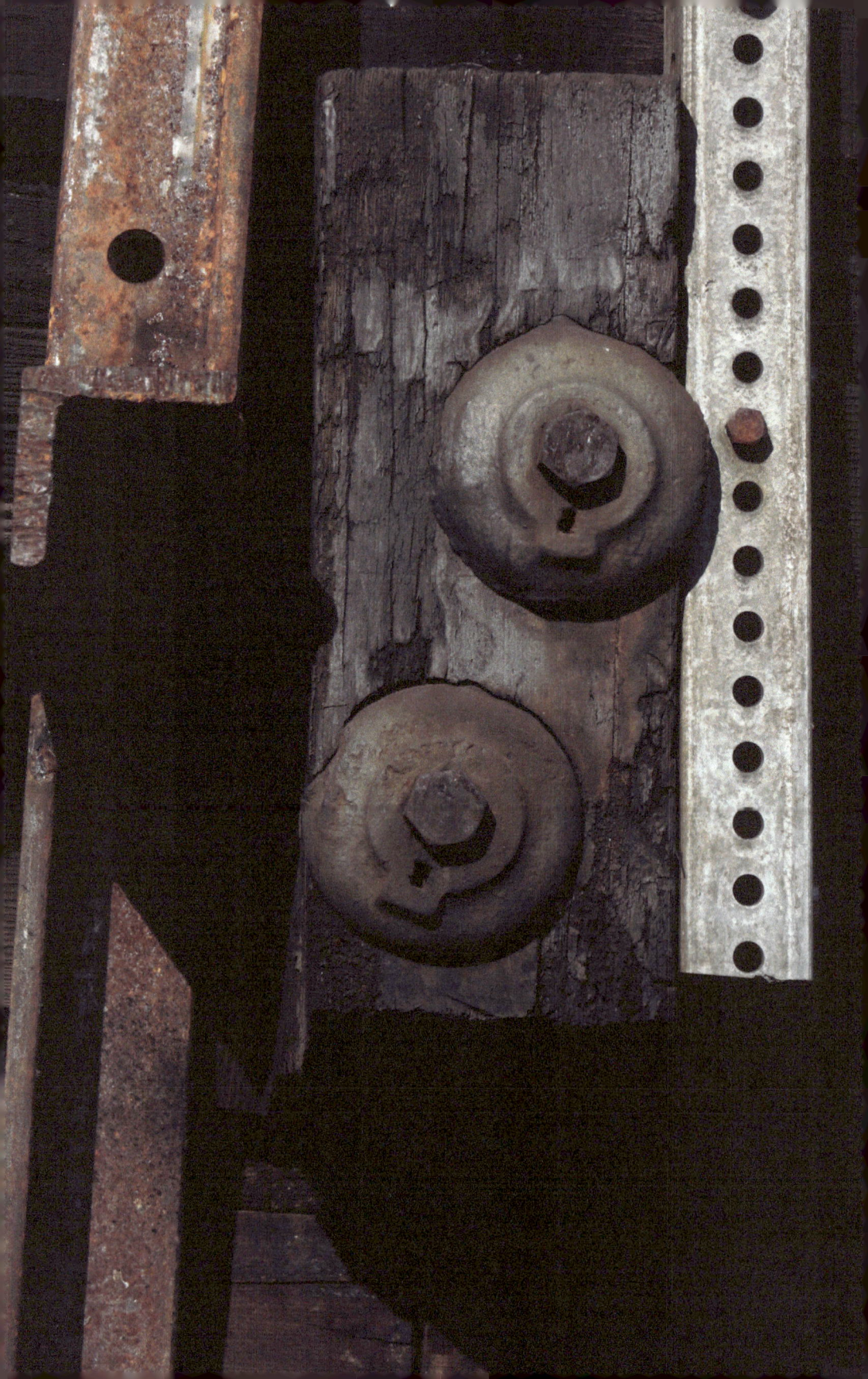

Sam didn't *feel* any different.
None of the passengers on the plane
looked any different.
He was even sitting in the same chair
as when he had started.
Nothing had changed.

After all that time and expense,
Sam thought that *something* would have changed.

What a letdown after all that
weighing, considering, and comparing!
All that time Sam had put into this,
and nothing had happened.

Sam couldn't believe it.

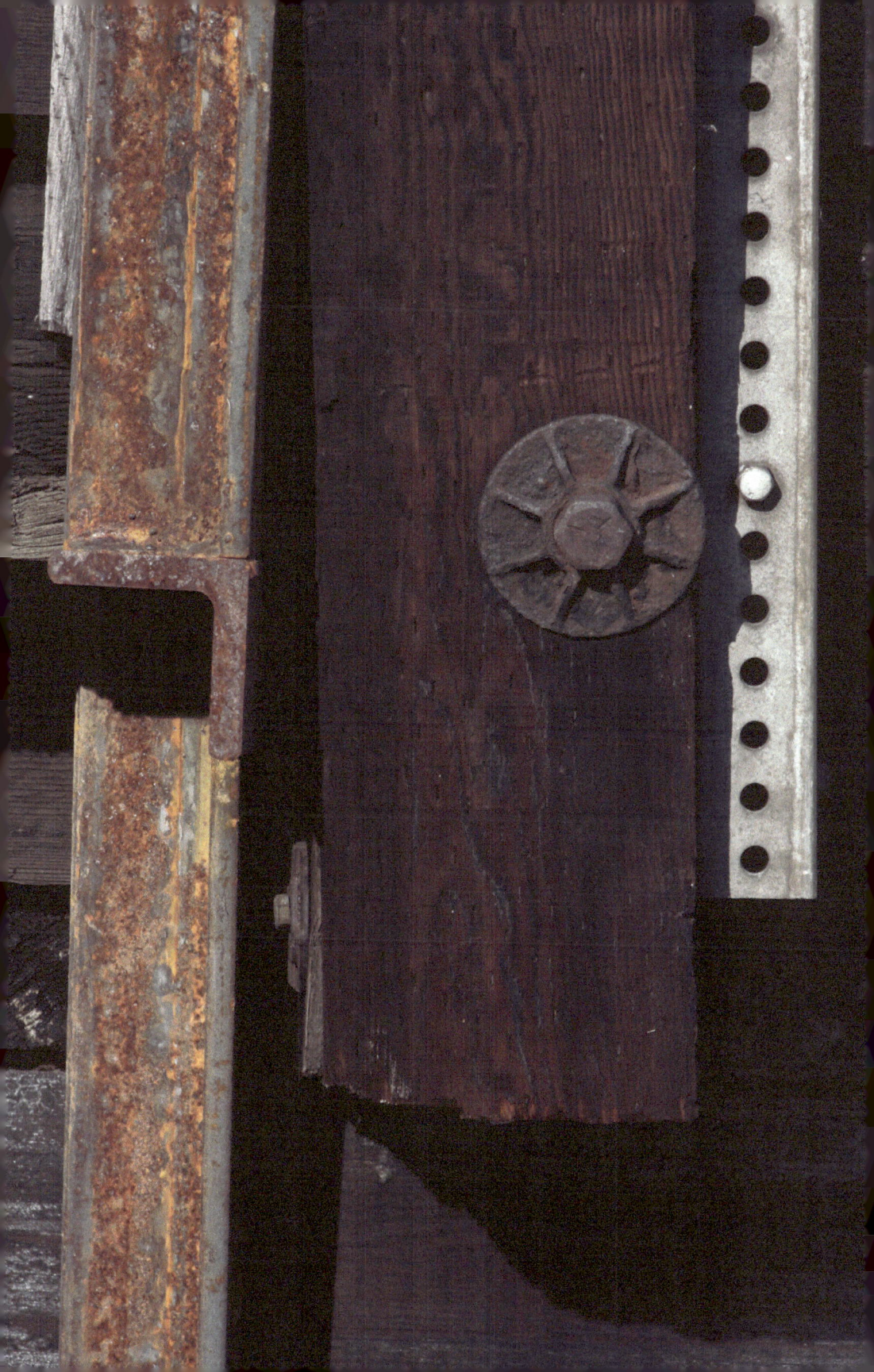

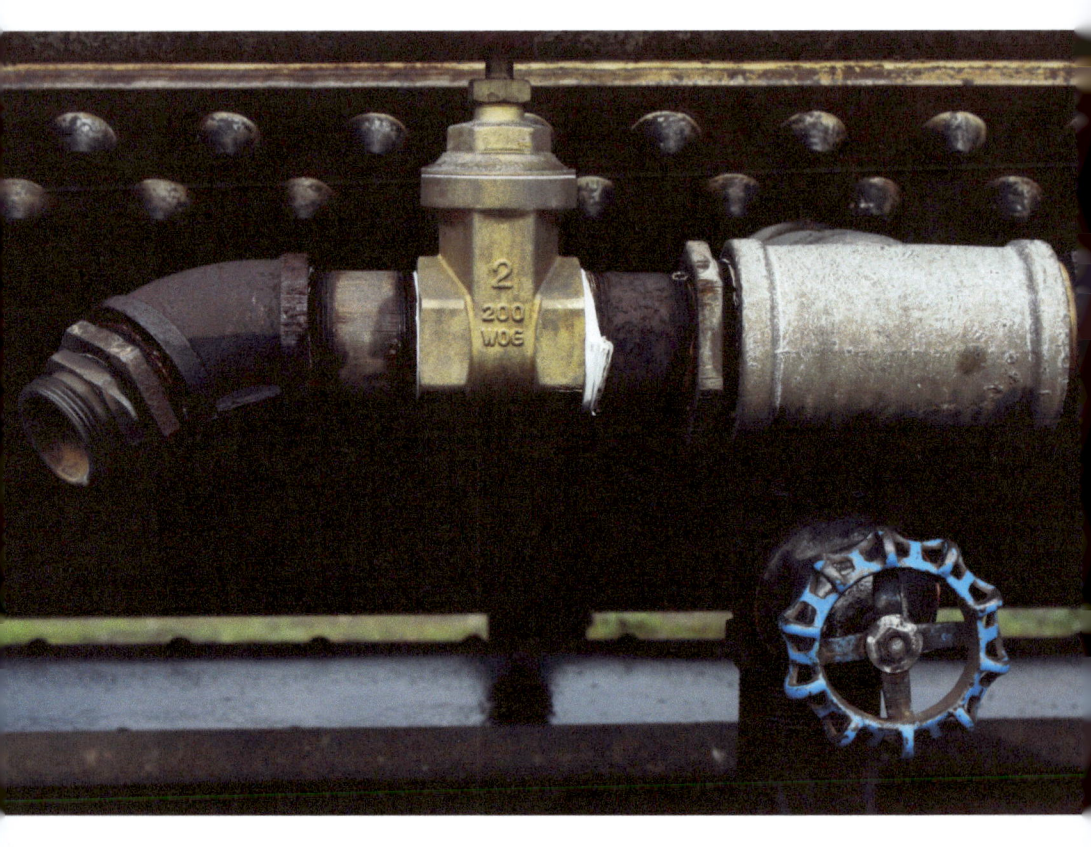

You may think that there *has* to be more to Sam's story, but there is not.

Sam stayed unhappy his whole life,
and he told everyone who would listen
how *disappointing* it was to ride
on an airplane:
all that planning and effort
and nothing changed when you landed.

Even if Sam never learned anything from his experience, maybe you can.

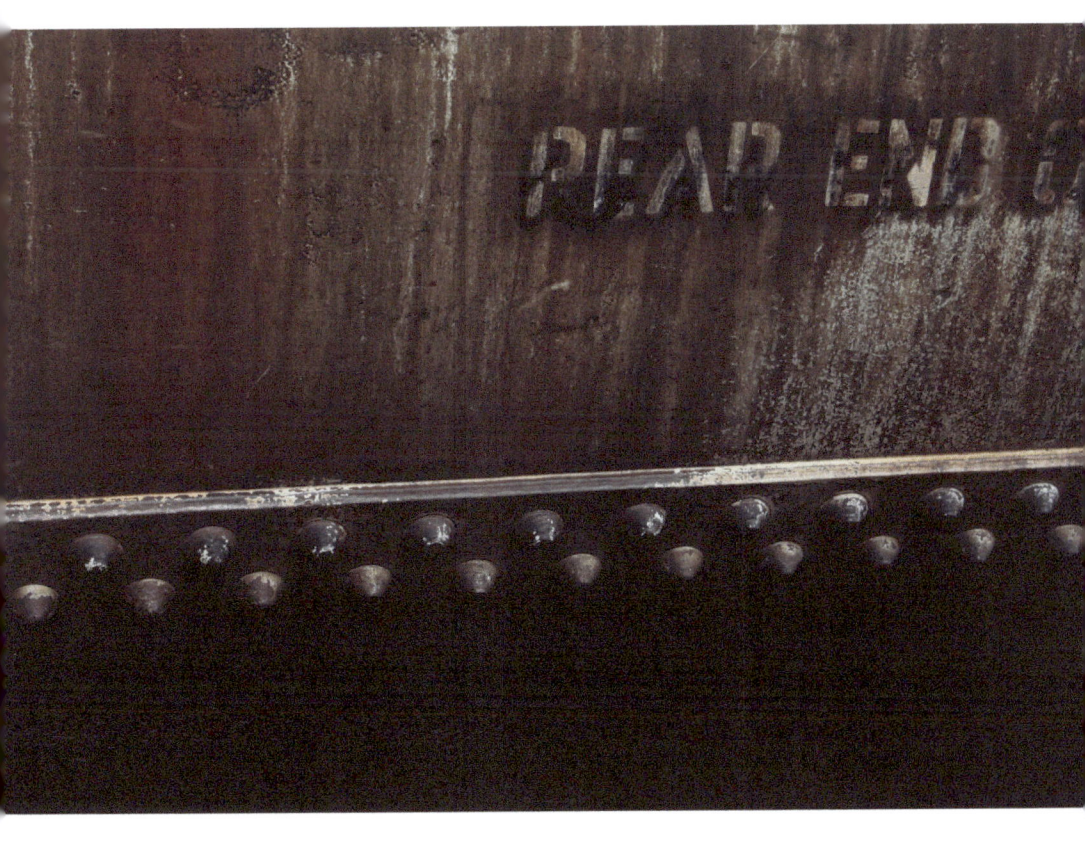

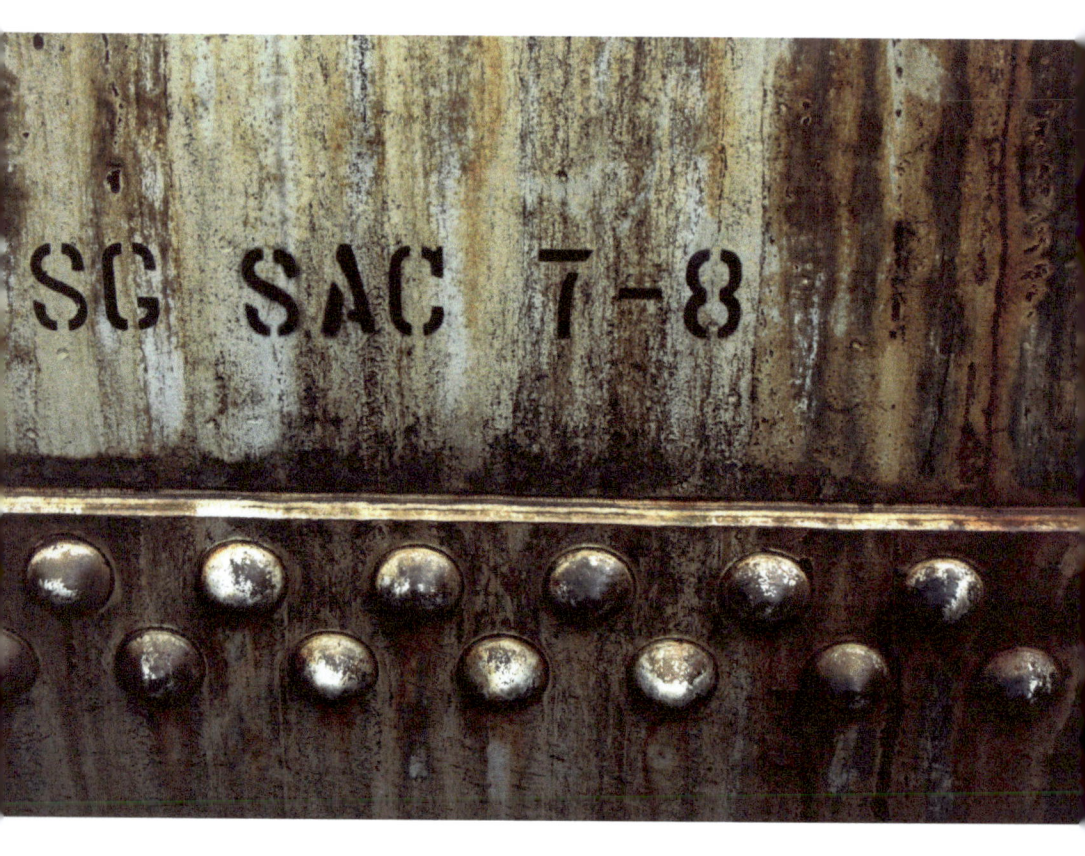

What has disappointed *you* in life?

How can you get off that airplane
and explore the possibilities
of the new place where you've landed?

~ ~ ~

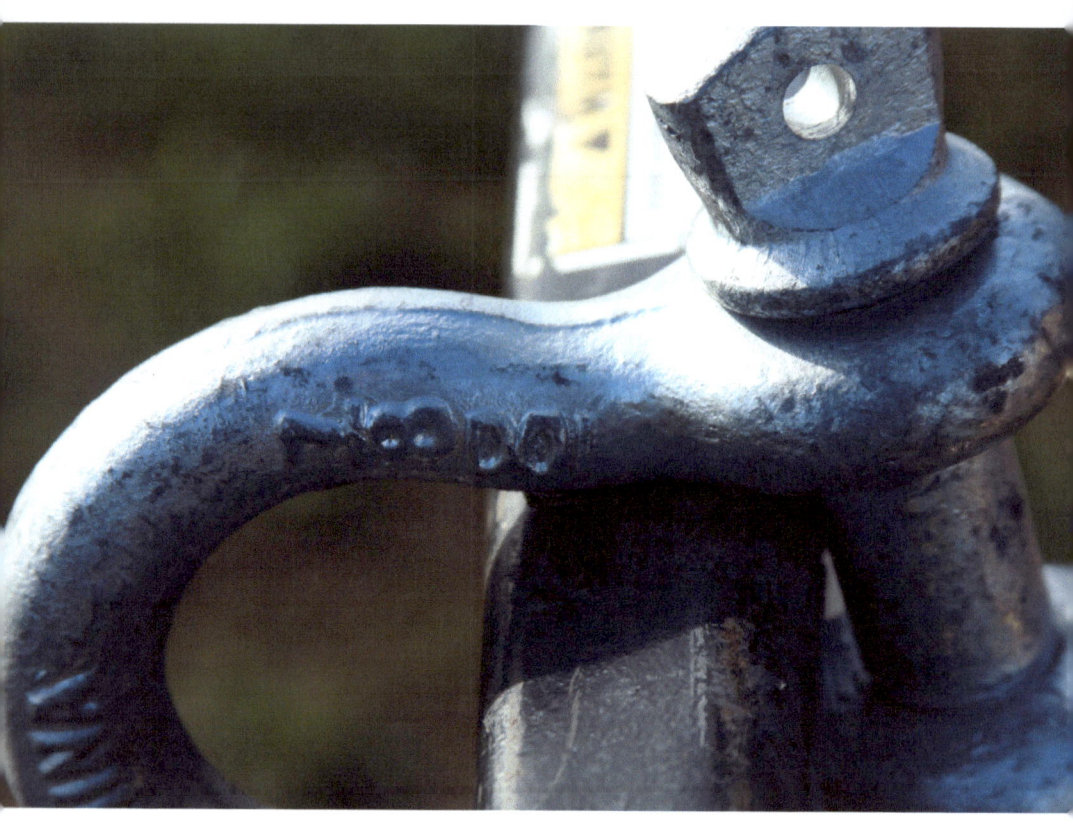

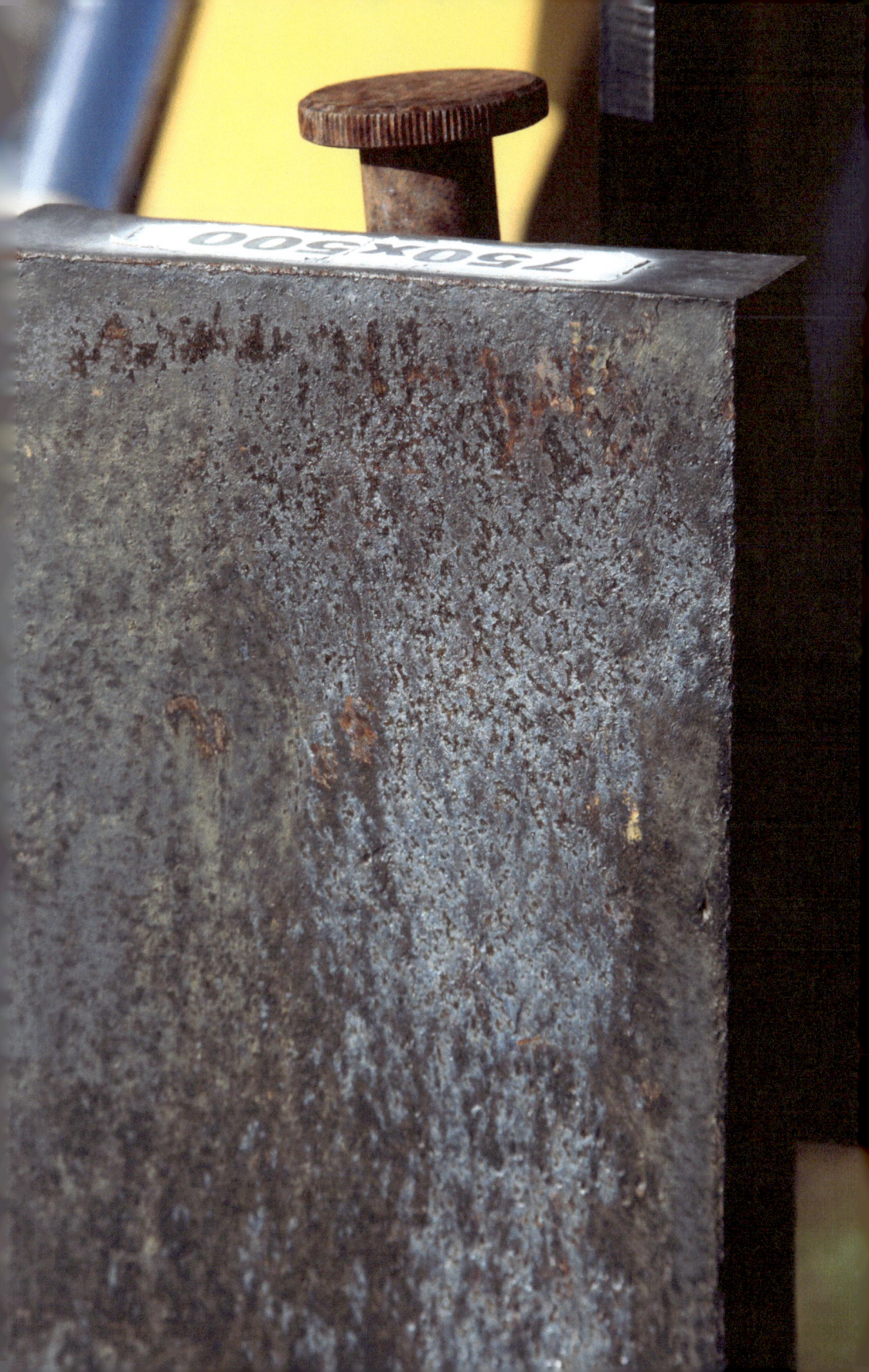

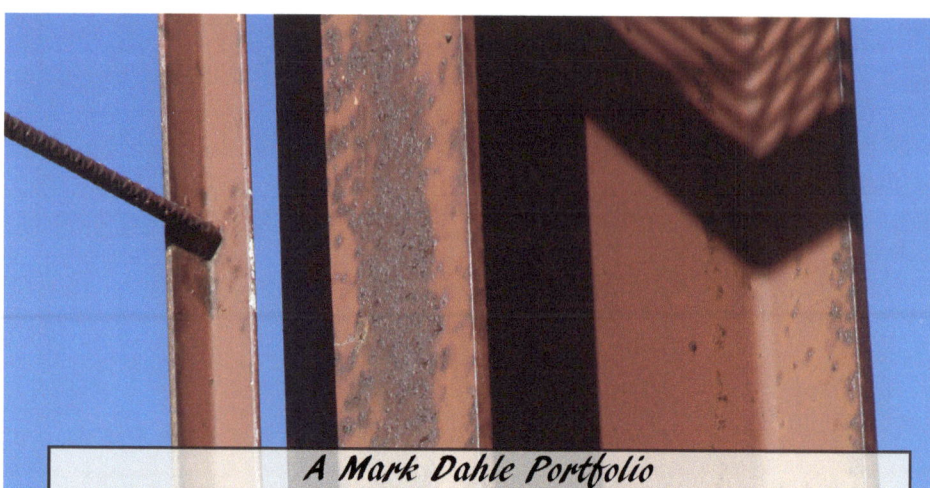

A Mark Dahle Portfolio

Race Day

This Mark Dahle Portfolio includes a beautiful painting, twenty-five outstanding industrial photographs from Minneapolis, and a story about a man going on a race (but picking up things to carry from the people around him).

What (if it's not too impolite to ask), what are *you* carrying that belongs to someone else?

Teri's
Renovation

This Mark Dahle Portfolio includes a painting, twenty-five beautiful industrial photos of New York, and a story about the renovation of Teri's house (which was a nightmare).

The contractor is an honest guy, so I'm certain he told Teri all the details, or at least some of them, at least in general. But maybe she wasn't listening.

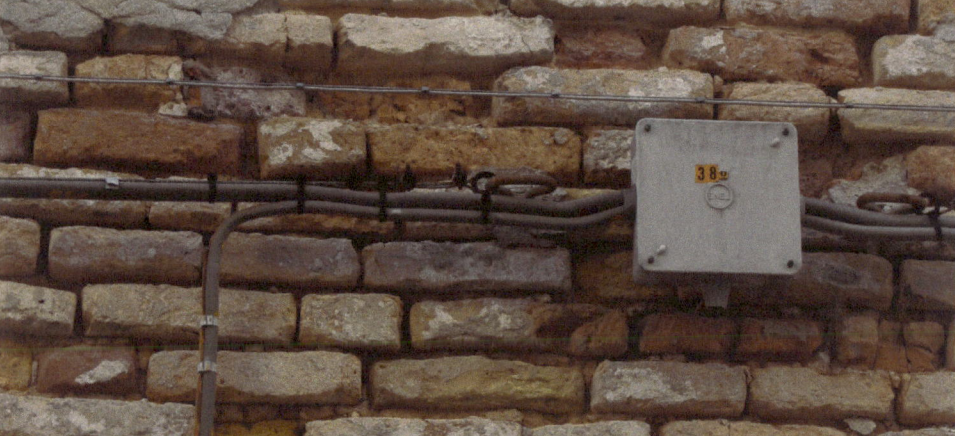

A Mark Portfolio

The Boy Who Loved Monopoly

This Mark Dahle Portfolio includes a colorful painting, twenty-seven beautiful photographs of Venice, and a story about a boy who loved to play Monopoly. One day the boy received $250,000 as an inheritance.

You probably haven't inherited any money this week.
But you've got lots of gifts
and lots of things that you're good at —
or could be, after you get more practice.
What will *you* do with all the gifts that *you* have?

www.ingramcontent.com/pod-product-compliance
Lightning Source LLC
Chambersburg PA
CBHW040853180526
45159CB00001B/411